I0749501

FACING THE CIRCLE

Facing the Circle

Carroll Blair

Aveon Publishing Company

(First edition, Mellen Poetry Press)

ISBN: 978-1-936430-20-8

Library of Congress Control Number
2012945807

Aveon Publishing Co.
P.O. Box 380739
Cambridge, MA 02238-0739 USA

Also by Carroll Blair

Grains of Thought
Reel to Real
Shifting Tides
Reaches
Out of Silence
Quarter Notes
By Rays of Light
Into the Inner Life
Gnosis of the Heart
Soul Reflections
Beneath and Beyond the Surface
Of Courage and Commitment
For Today and Tomorrow
In Meditation
Sightings Along the Journey
Through Desert's Fire
Offerings to Pilgrims
Human Natures
(Of Animal and Spiritual)
Atoms from the Suns of Solitude
Colors of Devotion
Voicings

Contents

Part I

Part II

Part III

Something Solid Please

Yes, in this maze of fuming nonsense
swirling without pause around the
swollen ankles of Life –

All corners ask for the same –
I speak for all – (that is, all corners).
We need something solid to
bite into . . . something even
to break our teeth on

What Grace Befalls

What grace befalls in sterile features
stunning cool hesitance with the light
of seven rainbows ten rules to a warning
lining up for a mercy killing for a fine of
tears spilling in the dust before a little boy's
joy rushed to blue saviors that've lost their way

Piece Offering

A thumb nail offers itself to a message
not yet clear, yet surprise is out of the question –
out of the reach of variables that have failed
in their abstractions sifting survivors from a
mind's battlefield — from its war-perennial
fighting for the Do or Die Parade

Center Z

All those impediments stinking nasty of haste
lacing wax for the dummies not yet frozen in time
still acting on impulse punishing the stars for the
flaws of light's speed arriving late to the bridge
managing peace between Now and Forever for a
treason's delight struck giddy for the rent of fire in
squared circles burning This and Thats into the story
of how zero came to be –

If Only

Can you see now what he's trying to do, the pink-nosed elf
stuck in traffic, cars bleeding steam forced into a ditch by the
glassy-eyed bitch who cares for nothing but the moon . . .
table talk in the wind scolding passengers with cracked
acorns in their teeth and stains of cherry on their toes
knowing nothing of the zillion invisibles swarming
around them, their minds too feeble to suspect –
They want to continue on their journey, that's all;
their journey to nowhere special for the sake of nothing real.

Can you see now what he's trying to do? The elf that would
be glad to save them – if only they were real

A Day's Reprieve

Such fine creatures not knowing themselves, not
gloating over themselves standing in bound innocence
sucking the genius from their jaws in sound ecstasy,
these saluted cows set aside for the day –
Nothing barred from the parasites that take their souls
in silence, sweet as the sour of their fate

Whole Delicate

Delicate words foreign to the ears of natures unrefined
so proud and stifling in their tents . . .

their lamps are electric –

fish are waiting to be gutted –

a swallow perched in the pine
waits for her share –

canoes like loaves of bread floating on
liquid silver, their time of rent is up –
            no merchants to guide them in . . .

laughter strikes the bush . . . a rabbit being mocked
misses the story of two nymphs naked in their conduct
released days ago by a woodsman changing his ways –

an owl follows the play in his sleep watched by brutes
from their tents waiting for the chance to steal his feathers
stuff them in their ears to block the sound of delicate words
cutting the wind invading the grounds, so torturous to crude
natures grounded holy in knave sin –

*   *   *   *

Words whole delicate out of here no (t)here, yes no-where
challenging brute hearts to open, to rise, to challenge themselves
in a game of soul descent, high noon beneath the stars

On the Way

Beaten down to the size of a stamp smothered in blood or a mushroom stew, a long-lost seeker finds his way to a cherub's pool, the night as cold as the day it has murdered. Twilight bleeps a signal to the gods and all hell breaks loose — *Hell*? I didn't know you existed (!) come join the feast of slaughter – Yes, No please, it's really no bother – a Japanese pilot rusty in his skills will take you to your room. I have prepared a dream to your liking . . . Heads will stand on heads and rock at your command (and roll if you want them to) and prayers will dance with Time and chain their children to your bed, and songs' still-sufferings will sing to their creators weeping in the room next to yours, its door locked forever – do you like tea or would you prefer dust and water? Oh no, please, it's really no bother; your devils are on their way

Questions Final

Can you not go on breathing a tad longer, just long
enough to place pad and pencil in your hands
so you may tell us the reason for your strife
and what you would do if it continued (your life)

The library's about to close

Is there something we can get for you?
Another bullet, perhaps

Heads Up

A sorcery of sorts prodded by a seminal gain diving up to a
weakened fox carried away unannounced, the rinse of fame
sweating in the street – a sneeze from the sucker parlor cuts
the air, no, there in the grass a light tames the frost singing to
arrivals, the pock-faced gluts all running in their minds to places
never seen not even imagined but (you know what I mean)
the jagged edge of everything crazy yes, I know but
spring knows something we don't – it doesn't want to be to
be the first one out of the block, the baby of seasons sporting
babies in the sun for a dream covered in fading snow – well,
you know; – or do you? What matters what's it matter
(Doesn't Matter!) So on with the tale of ghosts who will not
harm you unless of course you want them to and brave new
worlds ready to greet you, to carry you close to somewhere
frightening *to somewhere exciting* but do the roosters know
where you've been stringing nails like beads across the puddles
you like to call your seas angling red mornings assisting so
jealously the bloom sized for the ceiling-show where everything
bleeds in rhythms stuffed in the wink of time going without
shades but unseen just the same (do you see what I mean?)
a thorny gray's now moving our way – let's watch its coming (or
better) see where it is going (or better still . . .) see what it *wants*

Downbeat

A levelling down to levels unspeakable, to regions unbearable
to the eye to the heart to the soul – knaves in beaver suits
welcome at the gate crisp to a frozen core — the chore of
iodine puppets putting lice in the food to
to
to
to
to
to
and
and
(God you've said
a mouthful)

sipping deliverance from the broth of Lent soup

Know I — I Know

So claimed the man of No Regret seeping into the pores of guests
shown shackled by lean carriers abounding green around the table
(and did you see the picture of Sigmund on the mantle?).
Pipes mahogany-red feeding the calm of his fingers floating words
so cutting to the edge of the story prepared for yesterday's tomes
and the plight of zyme neophytes that've yet to have their say
cursing in silence, the voice without a soul . . .
the eyes without a face . . .

Benefit

Thrown to the dogs — a fielding of tubular groans
hatched complete in the heat of goal-ed arrangements
receding past star arguments, the protocol
twice down to the ball scraping dreams
from the brows of blind Pharisees
diseased in their intention to build sham cities
rising cageless to the sky

Tides of Entry

The unimportant phases out of tedium arguing the sunset maple
in its coming by stern gallantry stoned to blue needles, to left-
overs, to accumulated herring greased to the palmed frailness
of their bent, to signed authority training in pastoral space
to reach the orb of fusion narrow in its spleen . . .

A rude balancing surmounts counterwise to dutch callings,
and even now the harsh figures wash clean the elixirs crushing
their roots trying to bloom advanced to a standard of soiled
makeup, through blade rituals coffined in jeweled dread beyond
the order of futile rhyme tracing volatiles bound for siege

Going

Yes, gone to the long-fading courtesy sprawled uneven across
the field of a dying universe cognizant of its demise like no
living thing before it — a managing of sensibles stripped to the
quandary of descent forming inflections disorderly by orders
not meant for the interpretation of a scheme too prime to be
of use to Reality's fold stark to a naked See in Zen with the
artifice code of Life's assembly castling hard
the day that must end in betrayal

Flash of a Dream

A tree standing on its head,

its roots reaching for the sky;

the worms never so close to God

only for a second,

a moment,

a flash of a dream only

Recorded Recovery

A recorded recovery reflecting in the life of one L. Re-Covery dancing on the summit of Imagination the crowning jewel of humanity, when suddenly losing his balance a boy with a camera snapped his picture while flying in mid-air — the recovery of his spirit complete — only his body now needing repairs

What Have We Come To

What have we come to? Altars floating in dishwater,
they may as well be; – the roof of ancient beliefs caving in on
all corners of the heart . . . Aum-shares offered to the head
conquerors heading to their own illusions, trusting the
honor of their task like all noble fools on their way to
Nothing parading in the garbs of Something and Meaning
never forced to address the face of their fraud
always erecting new goats or gods to worship or
play with or admire or spit at — the sap of
false tales dripping from their chins

Metamotion

Floors steaming with mirrored pains fogging trails
to a stair-long secret . . . Teething pilots move to the window,
motion to the widowed snake fasting in the street curled in
solemn gesture hissing sweet poisons to ants and angels
praying silent for all truths killing in silence without name
(without love) without blame (without hate) without shame

Paradise

. . . just a stone's throw away;

but no one can find the stone,

and no one can see the way

Velocideed

Someone plug the hole quickly in the interior milky way
Life is breaking out at the rate of stoned holidays now escaping
behind the diamond cart designated for the trappings of lost
souls that barely hear the time melting around them pressed
to service agencies private in their peeking, the waxing of
foreign elders holding to laws unknown for the harbored
strife of cause ringing to effect back to running stages held
desperate to their fate for the charred remains of no
explanation willing and Willing to save . . . to wait . . .

As If to Say

He stands in the city street with a policeman on his back –
the horse, blinking his eyes and slowly turning his head,
caught in the bowels of civilization now crowding in the square;
its noises, its smells, its aggravations all in high pitch –
he dumps his breakfast in the street, snorts and neighs as if to say,
"That's what I think of your civilization," then proudly trots away.

Daily Report

A daily report of the goings-on in and around the world,
its ups and downs reported by mostly puppets and clowns
telling you what's important, what's newsworthy, what the
knaves are up to, what the fools have done and are now
planning to do, oh so important the news of the day —
local – national – world — the fleeting moments temporal,
caught up in events not worth your care today nor time
of day tomorrow.

P-h-o-t-o-g-r-a-p-h

People — so many people look at pictures of themselves
photograph after photograph
believing that what they are viewing is really themselves
is really who they are
believing they are looking at themselves, *seeing* themselves
when all the while (their lifelong while) their true being,
the genuine self lies laughing and weeping in a
corner of their soul beyond the reach of their senses
never to be found, never to be known

but my, how lovely you photograph

Show and Tell

The morning show presents a spot reserved for a song to be
sung by a gifted singer, composed by a worthy composer,
selected from a quality show now playing on Broadway
the best offering of culture they've had on since one can
recall – the song at the height of its delivery, the peak of
its power and beauty, cut off – replaced by commercials
of cars and batteries and credit cards, coffee and margarine
and other products too important to mention – the song
continuing heard at its beginning by millions, now sung to the
hosts and camera crew too busy preparing for the next
segment to take notice, the show now running behind.

Of course the bills must be paid, so they say, they always say
when these things happen, we should all know by now that
money is the bottom line, that things like this do happen, it
shouldn't be surprising – money upstaging art, yes, of course
(*of course*) – so why give it a second thought when few barely
give it a first

Integrity . . .

The bar of integrity dropping lower and lower . . . common
righteousness applauded as extraordinary courage,
speaking ever so loudly to the moral decay and
mediocrity of the age, of this age in the top ten of all-time
mediocre making the lists of most superficial, of most
decadent ever to manifest on the face of the earth
But how wonderful it is we have more television stations
to choose from and more stores than ever to shop in,
and more (we're told) on their way tomorrow
yes – how nice

Want I Want

A. “I want I want I want . . .”

B. “Yes, but what have you done you done for the things you
want you want, you home-of-the-brave
you born-of-the-free you”

So Easily

Sleeping
in
the
office
of
every
politician
of every
official

Disgrace

awakened
easily
(*so
    easily)*
by the
thump
of
a
crooked
toe

Capitol Thrill

He thinks his office important and himself, so very important
drawing the attention of those who think their job important
enough to point out the absurdity of his presumption of
importance, the media believing the story important enough
to air to the public who think it just important enough to pay
attention to for its value of entertainment, to read about or
tune in to with ear or eye and a little piece of mind, all involved
quite pleased with their involvement, the story sensationally
expressed (of course) sure to impress with all the air of
importance . . . with all the importance of airs

Special for the Nothing Specials

A main course of glory over-easy served with a
side dish of flattering BS and a beverage of ego-
stimulant guaranteed to make your pipe dreams seem
real as can be – also a salad of adore-you let-us
topped off with a slice of humbleless pie for dessert

Discounts daily for the vainiac who comes closest to
supporting his ego/vanity with genuine ability

Narcissus' Creed

Me me me I I I my my my us us us we we we our our our . . .
you see I must always be included in my thoughts, otherwise I'm
not able to think — yes, me or something to do with me or
something that will soon be having something to do with me,
though I don't mind sharing – no, really I don't; oh not in the
least . . . you can see this by my "us us's" and "we we's"
(and let's not forget "our") – but I can see nothing,
hear nothing, think or feel nothing that hasn't *something*
to do with me.   Sorry.

(Forgive me . . .   *I'm* sorry)

Togetherless

The Grade B's eyeing the Grade A's who despise the Grade C's, the Grade D's despised most by the teacher despised the most all together, now stuck with one another in a room with portraits of governors and presidents hanging from the walls, the window displaying the view of school buses lined up in twos waiting to transport the variety of humans with their host of differences from one freedom-prison to another to learn more golden rules, to be seated neatly in rows of two where some will sit and meditate while others sing the blues.

Know Surprise

The mailman rang the doorbell saying to the woman who opened the door handing her a letter "I think you may want to keep this," a letter from her daughter addressed to Santa Claus left in the mailbox, her seven-year old now at school, the woman saying thank you taking the envelope and closing the door, the letter asking Santa for gifts and toys for her friends and family and the poorest neighbors living next door asking nothing for herself except for the wish at the bottom of the page – that her mother loved her more.

From a Woman's Magazine

Every night thousands of women are raped in their beds
by the man they said 'I do' to

Custody

The child — a part of him, a part of her —
their union now severed — their fight now over
custody of the child . . . both wanting to leave the other
out in the cold as far away as possible — as far as the court
will allow —

Solomon on the bench looking for his sword

Prayer to Prayer

They leapt from prayer to prayer saying them quickly so
they could go out and sin again before dusk — and oh what
sins they could commit in the night approaching (it was Saturday)
and ask forgiveness from the Almighty Himself the next morning
without the middleman singing Hosanna in the Highest
the pages of his sermon out of order
Spiritus Sanctus   Amen

They missed Communion, of course, but
confession's next Saturday   2 to 4 P.M.

Last Request

All his life a non-believer, adamant in his non-belief
punishing to those who tried to convert him,
Sunday his best day of vice and sin, both family and
friends now amazed at the sight before them
he now lying in his coffin, lying at rest
his arms in the sign of a cross –

someone whispered "his last request"

The Widow

Not knowing what to do with herself after her husband died and
children all moved away, feeling lonely and bored with herself
she decided to go back into the workforce, still young enough
(only in her fifties) she studied to become a nurse, got her degree
and went to work (because she was bored, you see, not knowing
what to do with herself) and made her debut in her new
profession in quite a stunning fashion, giving two patients the
wrong medicine on her first day and by the end of the week
there were charts misplaced and changed by mistake, reports
missing and (again) she gave a patient the wrong medicine
this time killing the man, all because she was bored and lonely,
you see, not knowing what to do with herself

A Lamb’s Revenge

Fat splattering from the pan — the slaughtered flesh
taking its revenge on the one lusting to consume it –
four burns on the arms, two in the eyes and three on the hands –

Not bad for a leg of lamb

Happy Holiday

A holiday meal lying splendid on the table surrounded
by family members — the number of faces friendly
not the same for every member

Happy Holiday

Strangers Unaware

Conversing with someone who hasn't a strong sense of self-awareness is an impossibility, because you are never conversing with him or her, but what he or she thinks him(self) or her(self) to be, which is always an impostor unbeknownst to them, making the endeavor not only futile, but sad or farcical, depending on your temperament or way of looking at things (or her or him), and how many conversations pass between people unaware, having no idea of the unawares of those whom they are speaking to (and the unawares of them too) adding another error, just one more to the many expressing themselves, playing themselves daily in the perennial play of Human Folly.

As Punctuation

Lives, like punctuations . . . some are like exclamation points – the rarest – dancing on Life's summit . . . others like commas pausing and going with often not much showing – and others, like semicolons (longer pauses but sometimes beautiful, because . . .) and then the question marks, wandering in aimless directions without a hint or clue of who they are or what they should do – and the colons – forever preparing themselves for the extraordinary to happen that never happens, and finally the periods – never really starting, resting in safe havens rocking no boats and stepping on no toes.

Yes, lives as punctuations . . . perhaps there's something to be said about this . . . yes — something , ; : ! . (?)

Pamphlet from Somewhere in the Sky

Send all your complaints about the evils of the world to:

Human Behavior
Box 10001 Absurdity Drive
Planet Earth 60606

Never a Thought

Consider how many organisms are trampled on every day
by humans — giants to the insect world going about their
business, indifferent or oblivious to the life being crushed
beneath their feet . . . but they're only insects – nothing
of consequence – irrelevant to the needs of man . . .
pests, in fact – an inconvenience to the great children of
God . . . But kill a human being — oh, how evil (!) the most
horrendous crime imaginable (except in time of war, of course).
Now little can actually be done about the millions of
creatures being thoughtlessly murdered day after day
by the human species — but to never give it
so much as a thought . . .

something worth thinking about

What Would They Think

What would the animals think if they could reflect for a moment on all the holidays man takes for himself, makes for himself, and all the ceremonies created to celebrate himself (events of other kinds too, and life, occasionally, but mostly himself) . . . What would they think of how much, how *very* much he thinks of himself, thinking little for the most part about the rest of existence that surrounds him, too busy admiring himself, fluffing his feathers and blowing his horn . . . . If they could reflect for a moment beyond the moment upon this being that fancies himself the master of the earth and even the center of the universe . . .

if they could laugh could they ever . . .
if they could weep would they ever . . .   stop

For All His Faults

There are things about man that you just have to admire, that are truly amazing; like when his crazy dreams come true — his dream to fly, for example . . . those crude flying machines of the early twentieth century — the Wright brothers and other venturers pursuing their dream to fly like the birds they saw flying overhead ["If a bird can fly, why can't I?"]. From those sorry attempts trying without end to lift himself in the air, failing again and again, with sheer stubborn will and determination demanding of himself that he *will* fly . . . that he *will* lift himself into the heavens and see what the creatures of the sky are able to see . . . From those early days of feeble experiments to the landing on the moon in less than seven decades . . .

Amazing, man . . . truly amazing

A Moment's Influence

One moment following the next . . . the action it is sacrificed to as inevitable as the exhale following the inhale of a breath, placing its stamp before its brief existence has vanished on every moment that will follow . . . on every thought, feeling, gesture and motion of a life that ensues until reaching its final breath.

Ah the influence of a moment! How subtly it imbues its blink-of-an-eye destiny on the destiny of a life

From the Eternal Flame

Children playing in the schoolyard running about,
playing without care, without direction, with no
particular meaning or intent, lost in the rapture
of an abandoned bliss — seeds of humanity, or
something more . . . manifestation of something
greater, more encompassing spewing forth all
matter of Existence . . . they here, in recess,
now in this place, moving randomly about like
the atoms of which they and all there is are made –

Sparks from the Eternal Flame

Beneath Nature's Guiding Hand

a billion snowflakes ballet in the wind at a thousand
different meters, in a hundred different directions –

Nothing more graceful has man ever conceived;
has ever man done

At Once

A flock of birds darting from the tree
sending its leaves in flight
matching the birds' grace but
not their speed

Only So Far

the rising

    the vision

the journey on golden wings

Welcome to Science

. . . like when a beautiful theory is presented and many follow
based upon it — all correct, all beautiful, all fitting nicely with the
grand theory and then it's discovered that Papa theory is wrong
and the whole beautiful structure comes crashing down
egos bleeding in the rubble

welcome to science

Lost Dictionary

A dictionary of truths resting
in the light
on the seventh day
among leftover debris
the Creator sweeps away
(*all away* –)

truths (He believes)
the world must never see

Steady Boy Steady

Keeping the mind steady always steady when alone is difficult
or at least not easy, but the challenge is not the tightrope strung
tighter than a Norseman's bow forever hanging over head and
heart daring a spirit's walk, but the joy and fear flying overhead
with Love in their grip, whether to keep them in flight or allow
them to land, deciding which would be best, which would grant
the most challenging test to test one's measure of brain and
heart and what height might be allowed, the altitude proper
to raise the flag of courage rising from the soil of
steady boy steady

Challenge of Dawn

Every dawn arrives with a dare saying to man, "Give me your best shot, I'm only a child . . . I dare you to stay with me, to grow with me as I move from childhood to adulthood to old age and finally perish into the dark of midnight . . . I grow a life in a day — surely you can grow with me a little while I stay, while I am . . . surely a little . . . "

In Capture

The world capturing the mind, the mind, the world –
the result not always clear, not always known . . .
like the grip of two birds clinging to each other in
mate or battle falling from the sky

So He Believes

Your time of life is non-negotiable, but everything else
in and around it is

So man believes

The Journey Inner Like the Journey Outer

filled with space

with emptiness

with darkness

with abyss . . .

still (in both travels)
it is the only way to the stars

Emotionally Speaking

man has not left his cave;
has yet to leave the Stone Age

literally speaking

What the Hand Can Teach the Heart

and also the soul . . .

how to hold on;
when to let go

Eagle

From amazing heights he spots the life that will sustain
his own, coasting in full spread before making his descent
swift and sure to the surface of the sea, his talons
slapping its face in unison snatching his prey

the eagle lifting his silver prize flapping into the sun

Scene from the Zoo

They laugh at the animals behind bars — ignorant children
and stupid adults smug as they walk away not realizing that they
themselves exist in a cage though far more spacious, but for some
(perhaps for many) in a prison within more confining than that of
the animals so arrogantly mocked and pitied existing in their
cages who also see man behind bars, living and dying in his cage.

Strange World

What a strange world this would be if pigeons could birth eagles and lions, wildebeests . . . But alas, this can be done, and is so every day — by the human species.

Compass of Virtue and Vice

The compass of Virtue and Vice registering man's behavior
throughout history has always arrowed strongly toward Vice
and once there, resting comfortably while passing Virtue
jittery not quite settling, never staying for long
the arrow drawn to Vice most naturally, resting easy,
as if knowing just where it belongs.

S-e-c-u-r-i-t-y

Every generation goes about setting up securities for themselves
(castles in the air, really, not really securities) the artists and
thinkers of the day pointing out their fraud, their non-reality,
not to do harm or for the enjoyment of bursting the illusions of
innocence and innocents – no, not that — but so man may one
day have the courage, may find the strength to face the pains
of his existence; to confront his fear; – to live in the center of
Life's storm (the only *life* there really is)
and there to find . . . . security

Pastime

Passing itself off for something irresistible, for something
indispensable (yes) most essential to anyone who knows
something of the angst of everyone trembling in the shade
by the halftime of life blowing whistles not even dogs can hear

Of Mind and Body

The mind has its advantages over the body . . . this despite the body's marvel of design, its biological wisdom; – its wonders of defense and self-regulation . . . the mind can study the body, can talk to it, may amuse itself with the mass of flesh and bones moving about beneath itself . . . can tease it, belittle it, mock, if so inclined, its degenerative process, breaking down slowly, moving steadily toward its demise . . . can leave the body behind as it goes on flights of the imagination travelling to the ends of a universe and back and the body can do nothing, can't even talk back . . . but the body has a revenge, this one revenge, you see, that when the body goes so goes the mind, unless the mind goes first by madness or disease.

So mind depends on body totally for its life, but not its living, and body without mind? (you've got to be kidding)

Paradox of Pain

How strange it is, the paradox of pain . . .
'tis the thing that anchors man's spirit,
yet also gives it wings

Everything Lives to Sing Its Song

. . . to spill its love
or spew its venom
onto the pavement of
Life's unfinished Temple

Full — Filled

The world is filled with artificialities, compliments of
humanity — cement and tar, bug sprays and cars
complementing the quests of stale producers and
silent seducers hanging their dirty linen from sea
to shining sea

Now Addition

Little has changed in a way since the caveman left his cave each
morning going out to hunt prey to sustain his brood another day.
Now there are brutes in suits and ties going out hunting game . . .
knaves preying on fools thinking nothing of cheating and lying
if that's what it takes, whatever it takes to be a breadwinner,
to bring home the bacon, doing whatever they deem necessary
in the game of gather and gain to sustain themselves and their
families another day. (Not all, mind you, surely not all,
but enough to make this insight credible.)

Little change, really, beyond the following change since the cave-
man stalked his prey: — now women are also playing the game.

One to Wonder

What is the sum, I wonder, of all the illusions combined that occupy the head of every human being on the face of the earth? The number fluctuating, naturally, at any given moment . . . but the collective illusions of the human race that hold power over every dimension of its being; that wield so much influence over every human activity — every impulse, passion, motive and aspiration . . . . But what *is* their number, I wonder, say now at this moment jointly weaving the tapestry of humankind and shaping its destiny with no more reality than a dream –

If They Could Rise

If they could rise from their graves, all who have fallen in battle for a noble cause and see that what they had given their lives for is no longer, and the evils they had fought against are now again or surely preparing to rise in the future *again,* and witness how fleeting the hour of their victories, the monsters of man once more on the march or gathering force, relentless in their will to be; . . . . if they could see, these noble hearts, how temporary are even the greatest triumphs over villainy that many who have died for believed to be permanent like their fate of eternal sleep, their ultimate sacrifice most final for ideals that rise like the sun and fall like the rain . . .
yes, if they could rise from their graves and take a look around –
what would they think . . . what would they say . . .

Where to Now

From hunter to farmer to industrialist to computer hack,
on to the pinnacle of modernity madness.
Let every god and demon so ever conceived in all the world's
mythologies, fight it out amongst themselves
and tell man where he's off to now.

Lesson from Earth

The earth spins around at more than a thousand miles per
hour going nowhere but the same journey that takes it
three hundred and sixty-five days to travel and always
ending up in the same place spinning round and round,
making its journey around the sun at greater speed than
anything man has yet travelled by land, air or sea and
going nowhere, really, trapped in its groove of gravity.
So to all dear members of the human race hustling and
bustling about, running here and there, killing yourselves
to get somewhere believing it to be most important, the
most important thing in all the world, remember where
all this is happening — on the earth, spinning itself silly
going round and round, making the same journey
always ending up in the same place going nowhere,
really nowhere as it has for billions of years and
will continue to do so for billions of years more.

ABOUT THE AUTHOR

Carroll Blair is an award-winning author of more than twenty books. His work has been well endorsed and commendably reviewed, as illustrated by the following commentary from Midwest Review, which proclaimed, "*The poetic expression of Carroll Blair is both unique and compelling. Using word images like the strokes of a painter's brush, Blair creates a resonating recognition that is the mark of a master poet.*"
He is an alumnus of the Boston Conservatory and lives in Massachusetts.

www.ingramcontent.com/pod-product-compliance
Lightning Source LLC
La Vergne TN
LVHW050935080826
845145LV00004B/1276